Staffordshire
Bull Terrier

West Highland White Terrier

Dalmatian

German
Shepherd

Beagle

Jack Russell Terrier

GW00359401

King Charles
Spaniel

Smooth-haired
Dachshund

Smooth Coat Chihuahua

Bulldog

Greyhound

Pembroke Welsh Corgi

Pug

Labrador Retriever

Siberian Husky

Great Dane

Published in the UK by Scholastic, 2021
Euston House, 24 Eversholt Street, London, NW1 1DB
Scholastic Ireland, 89E Lagan Road, Dublin Industrial
Estate, Glasnevin, Dublin, D11 HP5F

SCHOLASTIC and associated logos are trademarks and/or
registered trademarks of Scholastic Inc.

Text © Ashleigh Butler, 2021
Written with Sally Morgan

Cover and interior illustrations by Risa Rodil © Scholastic 2021
Interior illustrations: Ashleigh and Pudsey p6.
Clicker Icon: 18, 44. Dog brushes: 17 & 40. Dog food: 38
Flea & Tick: 43. Vi, Sully & Eliza Icons: 23, 26, 31, 67, 85, 89, 90, 92

Interior Illustrations by Rachel Lawston © Scholastic 2021
Interior illustrations: 1, 8, 9, 12, 13, 14, 15, 16, 18, 19, 20, 21,
22, 23, 26, 27, 28, 29, 30, 31, 32, 33, 36, 37, 38, 39, 40, 41, 42,
43, 44, 45, 52, 54, 59, 61, 66, 71, 79, 83, 84, 86, 87

Basic Behaviours, Learning to Get Along, and Trickier Training
Instruction Illustrations by Jake McDonald © Scholastic 2021

ISBN 978 0702 31368 4

A CIP catalogue record for this book is available from the British Library.

Printed in the UK by Bell and Bain Ltd, Glasgow
Paper made from wood grown in sustainable forests and other controlled sources.

1 3 5 7 9 10 8 6 4 2

www.scholastic.co.uk

Ashleigh Butler

HAPPY PUPPY Happy Dog

How to train your best friend

📖 SCHOLASTIC

CONTENTS

5

INTRODUCTION

Hi! My name is Ashleigh, and I have been a dog lover since the day I was born. My mum loved dogs, too. From the age of eighteen my mum competed with all different breeds of dog in agility and flyball competitions. My mum was my inspiration and the reason I am where I am today. She taught me a lot, and even let me help train and compete with her dogs when I was just five years old! I loved it. After three years of competing with my mum's dogs, my mum and my nan decided it was time for me to get a dog of my very own. They saw an advert in the paper for a fluffy puppy and we went to see her the next day. I fell in love with Buffy right away.

Buffy was a fluffy little cross-breed (a Border Collie and Bichon Frise mix) and she was my best friend, but boy did she teach me a lot about dog training! Buffy had a strong personality and would only do something when she wanted to.

Buffy taught me how important perseverance and patience is when it comes to training a dog. Buffy was stubborn. Whenever I would ask her to do something, she would just walk off; when I tried to groom her, she would struggle to get away; when I threw a ball to play with her, she would give me a look as if she were saying, "Come and pick it up, then!"

Buffy wasn't perfect, but we learned a lot on our journey together and eventually, when she had puppies of her own, she gave me the greatest gift I could ever ask for. A beautiful puppy called Pudsey, who turned out to be my doggy soulmate.

In this book, I will share with you all of the secrets I learned from Buffy, Pudsey, Sully, Vi, Eliza and all of my very best furry friends. Find out:

- **How to decide which puppy is right for you and your family**

- **What to expect when you bring your puppy home**

- **What you need to do before you bring a puppy into your home**

- **How to care for your puppy**

- **How to tell what your puppy is thinking**

- **How to teach your puppy basic skills and behaviours**

If you read this book and it makes you want a dog even more, I am so excited for you because you're in for the best time ever. I can promise you if you stick with it, and keep putting that effort into training (just like I did with Buffy, **THE WORLD'S NAUGHTIEST DOG**) you will learn and gain so much from it.

Read on to learn everything you need to know about how to prepare, care for and become best friends with your new dog!

PAWS FOR THOUGHT

Puppies may be cute and irresistible but they are a big commitment. Your sweet little puppy may live for fifteen years! Before you decide to bring a puppy into your home, ask yourself the following questions.

- Do we have the time to give our puppy the attention they need?

- Who will take the puppy on walks?

- Who will look after my puppy if we go on holiday?

- Who in the family will look after the puppy if they're ill?

- Can we afford to pay for a puppy's medical care? (It can be expensive!)

Why Do You Want a Puppy?

If you want a puppy because you think they're cute and fun, but you don't feel like you want to put a lot of time and effort into them, perhaps it isn't time for you to get a puppy just yet. But, if you want a soulmate, a life partner who will give you unconditional love but will need a lot of your time and effort, you are in for a very exciting adventure.

GOLDEN OLDIES

Have you heard the saying, "You can't teach an old dog new tricks?" Well, I strongly disagree with this. Any dog at any age can learn something new, it's just about working with them and figuring out how they learn.

When my mum's dog Eliza turned five, I took her on as my own. I had never trained her myself and we didn't really have a bond or connection together. My mum had taught her some basic tricks and had also competed in agility with her, but our training methods and techniques were very different.

I started with basic things like spins, leg weaves and between position. She already knew some of these tricks, but it was about us getting used to each other. I spent time with her on my own, taking her for walks, playing with her. After we started to form a bond by doing basic everyday things, I then started teaching her new and harder tricks, figuring out what she liked, what she didn't like, and how quickly she learned certain behaviours.

When taking on an older dog, you are taking on the habits and behaviours that they have learned from someone else and their previous environment.

Today, Eliza and I have an exceptionally strong bond — she is loyal, hard working and dedicated to being with me — but I had to put that time and effort into her as soon as I took her on.

section 1:

PUPPY PLANNING

The best way to get you and your new puppy's relationship off to a great start is to plan ahead. In this section you will discover everything you will need to do before you meet your new furry friend.

PREPARE FOR THE UNEXPECTED

When people ask me what to expect when getting a puppy, I tell them to expect everything and anything! Just like you and me, dogs have different likes and dislikes, different personalities and different habits.

Before you get your puppy, make sure you do some research into which breed of dog would best suit your family. You need to be ready for anything, but doing some research into the breed of dog you are interested in can give you some clues as to what they will be like when they arrive.

WHICH PUPPY IS RIGHT FOR YOU?

A well-suited puppy is like a member of the family. Take a look at the people who make up your household to help you work out which puppy will be the best fit for your lifestyle.

Are you . . . always on the go?

If you are an active family, who love getting out and about, you will want a dog that can keep up with your busy outdoor lifestyle.

GO FOR: a dog such as a Border Collie, Labrador, Cocker Spaniel or Weimaraner. These breeds like nothing more than long walks and adventures.

Are you . . . happy homebodies?

If you live in a busy city, or know that you won't have lots of time to take your dogs for long walks, choose a calm dog that doesn't need lots of exercise.

GO FOR: a dog such as a Dachshund, Yorkshire Terrier, Cavalier King Charles Spaniel or Bernese Mountain dog might work better. These breeds are still plenty of fun, but don't expect you to put in multiple miles a day.

Are you . . . allergic to dogs?

Many people who are allergic to dogs are allergic to their hair and dander. Dander is a bit like dust, but is made up of tiny particles of a dog or cat's skin. If you, or someone in your home, is allergic to dogs, choose a breed that doesn't moult too much hair and dander. These are often referred to as hypoallergenic dog breeds.

GO FOR: some of the best breeds for people with allergies are Hairless Chinese Crested, Poodle, Yorkshire Terrier or Bichon Frise. Buffy and Pudsey were part Bichon Frise and neither moulted very much at all.

AVOID: German Shepherds, Pugs, Labradors and Siberian Huskies. Huskies have something called a double coat, which means they moult a lot, and all year round.

Once you think you have decided on the kind of dog you would like, ask your friends if they know anyone with that breed. People who already own dogs are a great source of information, as they live with their dog every day and know how much exercise they need, and how much it costs to feed them. They may even be able to let you know where you could get one just like theirs!

YOUR FAMILY TO THE RESCUE

A good place to learn more about which type of dog would suit your family, and even find one to bring home, is your local pet rescue centre. Many dogs and puppies in rescue centres were bought from breeders by people who didn't realize how much hard work and commitment it takes to look after them. Every puppy or dog that goes into a rescue centre is checked by a professional behaviourist to see which type of home would suit them best and whether they have any problems their new owners need to be aware of.

When you approach a centre, the people who work there will check you over, too! The centre will want to know as much about your family and your home as possible and what you are looking for in a puppy. This is to make sure that they not only find the right dog for you, but also the right home for the dogs they care for to make it less likely that any of them end up back in a centre.

Ashleigh's Tip

Many successful agility dogs I know were rescues! Just because they haven't had the best start in life doesn't mean they won't be the perfect pet for your family.

PREPARING YOUR HOME

When you have researched just the right puppy for your family and decided that you are ready to commit bringing one into your home, it's time to make sure your home is ready too. Gathering a few things for when your new friend arrives will make sure you both get off to a great start.

Brush

Puppies come with all kinds of wacky hairstyles. Some have long, soft hair, others have short, coarse hair, some have crazy, curly hair that tangles easily and some have no hair at all! A good brush will make sure your puppy is always looking and feeling their best.

Ask your vet, a local dog groomer or an assistant in a pet shop to help you decide what type of brush is best for your dog.

RUBBER/SILICONE BRUSH: A soft, flexible brush with large cone-shaped bristles. This brush is gentle on the dog's skin and can give a good groom as well as a bit of a massage. Perfect for dogs who do not like to be brushed, or can be used as a puppy's first brush to ease them into grooming.

SLICKER BRUSH: A brush with fine wire bristles that are packed close together. This brush is great for removing loose hair and getting rid of stubborn tangles from the coats of medium- to long-haired dogs.

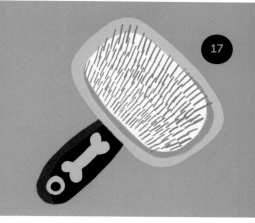

PIN BRUSH: This brush looks similar to a hairbrush you may have around your home. This brush is good for removing tangles from curly haired dogs that don't shed.

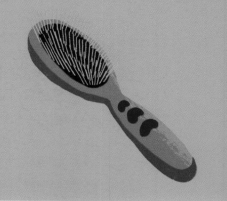

Crate

A crate is a safe and secure place for your puppy to settle down and rest – a bit like a den. A dog crate should be just large enough for your dog to stand up and turn around, and to stretch out while lying down. A crate is better than an open bed because it protects your puppy from wandering around freely and getting into mischief. A crate also means you can leave your dog in a room or in your home by themselves and know they won't be able to chew or destroy anything. Crates can also be used as a safe way to travel with your dog in your car.

Without a crate, a puppy can find it hard to settle, which could mean they don't get enough sleep. Being tired can make training difficult. A tired dog isn't able to fully focus on what you want them to do. They are more easily distracted and will switch off more quickly.

Ashleigh's Tip

When I'm training my dogs, I like them to be well-rested and keen to learn. I always try to let my dogs have a nap or rest in their crate just before a training session, so they come out fresh and ready to learn.

Blanket

If you are able to visit your puppy before you bring them home, take a blanket that smells of you and your home to leave with them. This will get them used to your smell. Then, when you bring your puppy home, bring the blanket too. The blanket will now smell not only of you, but also of where they came from. Place the blanket in your puppy's crate to give them something cosy and familiar to smell so they don't feel so lonely.

Food bowl and water bowls

You will need a bowl for your puppy's food and a few bowls for water. Putting water bowls around your home will ensure that your puppy can get a drink whenever they need it. Make sure to put a bowl of water in your puppy's crate in case they get thirsty between naps.

Collar and Lead

A collar gives you more control over your puppy than a harness. When you take your puppy to new places, they may get excited or worried, and a collar will prevent them pulling too hard on their lead. I prefer to have my puppies on a collar first of all as it's good for training and to prevent pulling; however, it can be good to move on to using a harness later on as it can be more comfortable for the dog.

Dog tags

Dog tags attach to your puppy's collar and should include your puppy's name, a phone number and your address. This information will help anyone who finds your puppy reunite you with them should they get lost. You could also include whether or not your dog requires any medication. You can have tags engraved in many pet and hardware shops.

Safe car travel

Under UK law, dogs travelling in cars must be able to do so safely either in a crate or secured with a doggy seatbelt. This is both for your puppy's safety and yours, so it's a good choice wherever you live. Ask your vet or an assistant in a pet shop to help you choose what is right for your puppy.

Puppy/dog food

There are lots of different types of dog food. Ask, when you visit your puppy at the breeder's home or in the rescue centre, what type of food they are used to so that you are able to offer your dog some familiar meals when you bring them home (see page 36 for more information).

Toys

Buy a range of toys so that your puppy can decide which are their favourites. A variety of toys, as well as being lots of fun to play with, will hopefully distract your new puppy from wanting to chew on things they shouldn't!

There are lots of things that puppies shouldn't chew. Most people think throwing sticks for dogs is good fun, but it can be quite dangerous. If the stick splinters, sharp pieces of wood can hurt your pet's mouth.

Puppies love toys, but they can't tell the difference between toys which belong to them and which belong to you. Keep your toys out of reach of your puppy, especially small toys that they could swallow or could get stuck in their mouth.

Ashleigh's Tip

Puppies love to chew! Make sure you keep anything that means a lot to you out of their way! Put shoes, bags, toys and favourite stuffed animals away somewhere up high or in a cupboard so they can't reach them.

My young Border Collie Vi is terrible for chewing, including the wires in our van, resulting in a repair bill of £200! Luckily, Vi was fine, but now I make sure that everything he could possibly chew is nowhere near him. I also don't buy my dogs anything too expensive, so if they do happen to chew something such as their bed it doesn't matter too much.

An appointment at the vet

A good vet can help keep your puppy happy and healthy. As soon as you know when your puppy will arrive, ask an adult to make an appointment at your local vet. Vets can get very busy, so making your appointment early will help to avoid long waiting times. The vet will check your puppy is in good health and give your puppy vaccinations to protect them from diseases. The vet will also fit your puppy with a microchip. This microchip has a unique number which, when scanned, can help anyone who finds your dog, when they are lost, to contact your family. In the UK, all dogs who are older than eight weeks must be fitted with a microchip by law.

Once you have everything your puppy needs and have made their veterinary appointment, it's the moment you have been waiting for – it's time to bring your puppy into your home.

Section 2:

GETTING TO KNOW YOUR BEST FRIEND

Congratulations! You have a puppy of your very own! What next? Now it is time for you and your puppy to get to know one another. Read on to discover just what your puppy is thinking and how to learn to get along.

WELCOMING A NEW PUPPY INTO YOUR WORLD

Do you remember your first day of school and all the emotions you had when meeting your new classmates? You may have felt shy, nervous, sad and excited all at the same time. That's how your puppy is feeling, but they can't tell you that in words. Follow these top tips to make sure your first few days with your puppy go smoothly.

keep it simple

Try not to overwhelm your puppy. It's daunting for a puppy to leave their home and the life they have known for the past few months. When you bring them into your home, don't have too many people there to meet them. Try just to have the people who live in your household and who will make up their new family.

Follow your puppy's pace

Don't force your puppy to do anything they don't feel like doing. It's natural for you to be excited, but try to stay calm. Don't worry if your puppy doesn't want to eat or to play with you right away, that's absolutely normal. It might just take them a bit of time to get used to you.

When I first brought Sully home with me, he was very timid and decided his safe zone was the sofa, and he didn't move from that spot for a good while. I didn't force him off or pick him up and move him somewhere else, I just waited patiently. I kept approaching him, giving him a little stroke, showing him that I was a nice and fun person to be with. Eventually, he shyly jumped down from the sofa and joined me on the living room floor. After that he was playing tug with me, running around crazily and making the place his own.

Every dog is completely different. Some puppies might come into your house and act as if they have been there their whole lives. If this is the case, then you can start introducing new and exciting things to them straight away: their new toys that you have bought for them, their food and water bowls, their new collar, and so on.

Get outside

Show them the garden if you have one. Going outside with them will help to keep their confidence up and they will be more likely to explore.

Be gentle

Make sure that you are gentle when you are handling and playing with your puppy, especially if you are playing tug. A puppy's teeth can be sensitive.

POTTY TRAINING

Older dogs, and some puppies, may come from the breeder or rescue centre already house trained; however, others might not. Potty training can be tricky, so this may be where opting for a slightly older dog may suit you and your family more.

When house training, for the first few weeks you need to get your puppy outside as much as possible to ensure they go to the toilet. I try to take my puppies outside every two hours come rain or come shine and through the night, too. Taking them outside and making sure they go to the toilet helps to eliminate indoor accidents.

BECOME A BODY LANGUAGE EXPERT

Ever feel like you know exactly what your best friend is thinking without them ever having to say a word? You can do the same with your puppy! A good way of getting to know your puppy is paying attention to how they behave. Being able to read your puppy and their body language is very important because this how your dog communicates with you.

Look out for these subtle signals to find out how your puppy is feeling and to make sure you and your furry best friend are always on the same page.

Is your puppy . . .

- Wagging their tail?
- Barking or whining impatiently?
- Jumping up at you or up and down in front of you?
- Running in all different directions?

Your puppy is: EXCITED!

It's important to try and be as calm as possible while your puppy is excited because you don't want them to become overexcited. Young puppies may even wee a little – they should grow out of it as they get older! It might be funny to see them acting crazy at first, but being too excited can lead to behavioural problems and make your puppy hard to control.

Is your puppy . . .

- Breathing/panting heavily?
- Yawning?
- Licking their lips?

- Shivering?
- Hiding?
- Not coming when called?

Your puppy is: WORRIED

If you think your puppy is worried, try and be as calm as possible. Don't force your puppy to come to you. Instead, give them some space. If you suspect your puppy is worried about new people, let them spend some time alone in their crate.

When your puppy does come to you, stroke them with long, slow strokes down their back. This will reassure your puppy that you are there, you are calm and that you are connected with them.

If your puppy is nervous while you are out and about, speak to them calmly and use treats to keep their attention on you and distract them from whatever is making them nervous. If this doesn't work, remove them from the situation and try another day.

When meeting new people, don't force your puppy to socialize. Ask someone to give them a treat, tell them to try not to give them too much eye contact, or be too animated. A lot of people make the mistake of being too pushy or excited when meeting a new puppy, which some dogs can find scary.

Ashleigh's tip

If your puppy is nervous a lot, keep a record of when and where you are when it happens. This will help you pinpoint exactly what it is that is making your puppy feel this way. Once you know, you can work with your puppy to help them feel more comfortable.

Sully was scared of the whole world when I first got him, especially people, but I never forced him to say hello. I kept his focus and attention on me so he didn't even notice the other people. Once he started putting his trust and confidence in me to not put him in situations he wouldn't be able to cope with, he started learning that people weren't that scary.

Is your puppy . . .

- Forgetting their manners and how to behave?

- Acting like they can't control their body?

- Running all over the place?

- Biting or nibbling you?

- Drinking more than usual?

Your puppy is: OVERTIRED

Sometimes behaviour that looks like your puppy is excited could actually be overtiredness. As you get to know your puppy, you will soon be able to tell the difference. When your puppy is overtired, ask them to go to or take them to their crate/bed so that they can get some rest. They might protest the first few minutes, but persevere and they'll be asleep in no time!

Is your puppy...

- Whining constantly?
- Chewing out of frustration?
- Stomping their feet?

Your puppy is: HUNGRY

Make sure you do your research on how much your puppy or dog should be eating at their age, but remember this is just a guideline and every dog is different. I find it very important when I first get a dog to set a routine for them, especially for food times. This way you can keep track of how much they are eating and whether or not they may need a bit more.

Is your puppy...

- Giving you their full attention?
- Wagging their tail?

- Barking confidently?
- Trying to engage with you?
- Giving you eye contact?

Your puppy is:

ENTHUSIASTIC AND READY TO LEARN!

I always try to make sure my dogs have had a nice rest before a training session. I let them out to go to the toilet before we begin. This is important as I don't want to start a session and discover my puppy can't concentrate because they need the toilet!

Section 3:

CARING FOR YOUR PUPPY

An important thing every new puppy needs to learn is that they can trust you to do your best to care for them and keep them safe. Inviting a puppy into your home is similar to inviting friends and family over to visit: you want to make sure they are as comfortable as possible by giving them somewhere warm and clean to stay, fun things to do, and delicious, healthy food to eat. Follow these top tips to make sure your puppy knows they have found their *furrever* home.

FRESH BED

There is nothing nicer than settling down in a nice clean bed after a busy day, and your puppy likes this too. Make sure to keep your puppy's crate and sleeping area clean. Cleaning your puppy's bed regularly will help keep your puppy smelling fresh, too.

Ashleigh's Tip

If your puppy settled down in their bed when they were wet, make sure you clean it after. Wet dog smell is the worst!

WHAT'S ON THE MENU?

The most important thing to look out for when choosing food for your dog is good quality ingredients. If choosing pre-packaged food, such as kibble or canned dog food, make sure to read the label carefully. Dogs need plenty of protein, so make sure the first ingredient listed is meat, such as fish, chicken or beef. Some vegetables are good for dogs too, but avoid foods that contain grain, which may be good for you and me but is not good for dogs.

Feeding your puppy the right amount of food is just as important as what you are feeding them. When I first get a puppy, I feed them four meals a day. Young dogs have littler tummies, so it is important to feed them small meals regularly to make sure they get all the energy they need to play as well as to grow strong and healthy.

All of my dogs are raw fed, which means I feed them muscle meat, meat still on the bone, vegetables, fruit and raw eggs. I love how natural raw food is for my dogs. I think it makes my dogs healthier and find it gives them lots of energy and a glossy coat.

Ashleigh's Tip

Feeding your puppy a raw diet will make them produce smaller, less smelly poos!

A raw diet is a healthy choice for your dog; however, there are some drawbacks.

Raw food needs to be kept cool to stay fresh. I have a separate freezer for my dogs' raw meals, and I have to make sure I remember to defrost them or they won't have anything to eat. Also, when using a puppy's meals for training, it doesn't always smell very nice.

Finding somewhere to keep your dog's raw food when you go on holiday can be very tricky.

NO QUIBBLES WITH KIBBLE

While I prefer to raw feed my dogs, it's not the be-all and end-all. Many people feed their dogs dry food called kibble and find that not only do their dogs enjoy it, but that it keeps their dogs healthy and gives them all the energy they need.

Treats and snacks

The treats you use should have the same nutritional value as your dog food. As I raw feed my dogs, I look for treats that have ingredients and nutrients as close to raw food as possible. This will help your dog's gut health and make sure its body doesn't have to adjust to different foods all of the time.

Ashleigh's Tip

Whatever food you choose to feed your dog, make sure to keep your dog's food and water bowls clean so they aren't picking up any nasty bugs or bacteria.

Forbidden Foods

Most human foods aren't good for dogs as they are too rich and fatty and can give your dog a poorly tummy, and sometimes cause even more harmful health issues. In fact, some foods you find delicious can be very dangerous to dogs. Make sure to keep all of these foods well away from your puppy. If your puppy does accidentally eat any of these, then get them to a vet as soon as possible.

- **Chocolate**
- **Corn on the cob**
- **Avocado**
- **Grapes and raisins**
- **Onion and garlic**
- **Cooked bones – they can splinter when your dog chews on them.**
- **Macadamia nuts**
- **Salty foods**

WALKIES

Taking your dog for a walk is great not only for your and your puppy's physical health, but also for their mental health. Puppies who don't get enough exercise can become anxious and stressed and start to develop bad behaviours such as chewing and barking.

Ashleigh's Tip

Take it slowly. Very young puppies need lots of rest. A five-minute walk, twice a day is plenty. Puppies are still growing, so you need to take care not to stress their delicate joints and bones. As your puppy gets older, add five minutes to their walk time for each month.

BASIC GROOMING

Grooming is an important part of caring for your puppy. It is a great way to bond with your new best friend and it also helps keep them healthy and comfortable. It helps them look and feel great, too. Think about when you're really dirty and mucky and then go and have a bath. Don't you feel so much fresher after? It's the same for your dog.

Get your puppy used to grooming straight away so it's not a foreign activity for them. The earlier you introduce it to them, the calmer and less stressed they will be when it is time to reach for the brush.

All dogs need regular baths and grooming at home, but some dogs with coats that are trickier to take care of, such as Poodle and Poodle crosses, Spaniels, Tibetan Terriers and Schnauzers, may need to go to a professional dog groomer to help with their grooming and coat upkeep.

Great reasons to groom:

- **Detangling a dog's coat helps it to grow healthy and strong.**

- **It makes your dog feel fresh and ready for anything.**

- **It helps you to bond with your dog.**

- **It's a great way for you to check your dog to make sure they are in good condition.**

Things to look out for:

MATTING/KNOTS IN YOUR DOG'S COAT:

These can be really uncomfortable for your dog. Regularly grooming with a suitable brush will help keep your puppy's coat tangle free.

DIRTY/HAIRY INNER EARS:

Check inside your puppy's ears to see if they are dirty, especially if your dog has big or floppy ears such as a Spaniel or a Cockapoo. Dirt left inside the ears can cause an infection. I find the best way to clean a dog's ears is to use a cloth and some warm water. Also, some dogs can get really hairy ears which can trap bacteria and affect their hearing. If your dog gets very dirty or has very hairy inner ears, ask your vet how best to clean or trim them.

EYE GUNK:

When you wake up in the morning, do you sometimes have those little eye bogeys that you have to wash off of your face? Dogs get eye gunk too. Keep your puppy's eyes clean by wiping away any goop with a clean, damp cloth. If you notice your dog has a lot of eye gunk, and you are clearing it more often than normal, you may need to take them to the vet as it could be a sign of an infection called conjunctivitis.

PAW PADS: Injuries to paw pads are very common. Check your puppy's paws and trim away any excess fur underneath and around their pads. Keeping the fur away from their pads can help keep them clean and healthy, and stop them from holding on to dirt and mud. Always ask an adult to help you before trimming your dog's fur.

NAILS: If your puppy's claws get too long, it can become uncomfortable for them to walk. Also, if your puppy's nails are very long, it makes it more likely that a claw could get ripped off, which can be very painful for them. Walking your puppy or letting it run on concrete (for a short period of time) helps wear their nails down a little, but make sure to keep them neat and trimmed. If you're not sure how to trim your puppy's nails, take them to a local dog groomer and ask them to show you how. And always ask an adult to help before trimming your dog's nails at home.

BATHING

Giving your dog a good wash in the bath or shower not only keeps them smelling fresh, but it also helps to keep their coat and skin healthy. Giving your dog a bath also gives you the chance to check that they haven't picked up any nasty bugs such as ticks that need to be removed immediately.

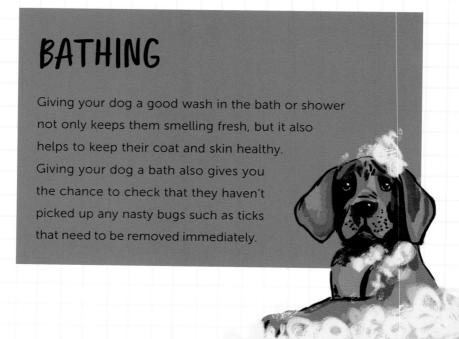

PUPPY PARASITES

Parasites are small creatures that can live on or in your dog and cause them some big problems. Common parasites that would love to feast on your furry friend include fleas, ticks and worms. These parasites can cause your puppy to have behavioural problems. You try learning something new when you are itchy all over because you are covered in fleas! It can even make your puppy very sick.

Speak to your vet about which flea and worming treatment they would recommend for your dog. This is important as different breeds of dog need different medications and dosages.

LEARNING TO LEARN

As soon as your puppy has settled into your home, begin teaching them how to learn. If you can activate that learning process in their brain, it will make your life a lot easier and make training a lot more fun for both of you. One method I like to use is clicker training. A clicker is a small plastic device which makes a clicking sound when you push a button.

You can use a clicker device to let your dog know that you are happy with something they have done and reward them with a treat.

Ashleigh's Tip

If you are always talking to your puppy, telling them they are a good dog and cute, it makes it much harder for you to mark a particular behaviour that you want them to do. With the clicker device, they should start to learn very quickly that when they hear that click, that equals a reward. That should hopefully lead to your puppy thinking, "What I did just then gained me a click and reward. If I do it again, will I get another one?"

SHAPING YOUR FUTURE FRIENDSHIP

For a lot of behaviour and trick training I use a method called "shaping". This method is based on waiting for your dog to offer a behaviour, marking it with the clicker and then rewarding them. By using the shaping method, I've found my dogs start to pick things up more quickly, offer behaviours or tricks on their own, and are thinking for themselves rather than waiting for me to show them what to do.

Ashleigh's Tip

The most important part of shaping is the rewarding. Be careful to make sure you are rewarding the correct behaviour as soon as your puppy shows they can do it. Rewarding too late will confuse your puppy as they won't be sure what they did to get a treat. This may lead your puppy to pick up bad habits.

For example, if you are waiting for your puppy to sit and they offer the behaviour, but you don't click and reward them until they stand up, instead of teaching your dog to sit, you have taught them to sit and then stand up again. This means when asking the puppy to sit for a longer duration they will find it hard as they have always sat and quickly stood up.

section 4:

YOUR PUPPY'S FIRST LESSONS

Now that you and your dog know each other a bit better, it is time to get to grips with some basic training. Read on to discover how teaching basic behaviours can be fun for both you and your pup.

BASIC BEHAVIOURS

These basic behaviours are some of the first things your puppy needs to learn. Practising them with your pup will ensure they become a best friend you can rely on. Follow these simple steps to have your puppy eating out of your hand.

Ashleigh's Tip

When training my puppies, I try to remember that everything is just a game to them, and I make it the most fun thing ever!

BASIC BEHAVIOUR : SIT

Sit is a great first command to teach your puppy because it is a natural behaviour which you can use to your advantage. I teach the sit position early on as it is a clear, stationary position for my puppy. If I want them to stay still, be calm for a few seconds or keep their attention on me, I usually ask them to sit as it stops their movement.

YOU WILL NEED:

- Clicker
- Treats
- Toys
- A bit of patience!

1. Stand up straight with your puppy in front of you.

2. Stretch out your arm and hold out a treat so it is just above your puppy's head. (Not too high as then it might encourage your puppy to go up on their back legs.)

Click!

3. If your puppy jumps up to get the treat, try not to say anything. Reset their position and start again.

4. As soon as you see your puppy put their bottom on the floor, click the clicker and reward them with a treat. If your puppy stands before you have a chance to give them their treat, do not offer the reward.

BASIC BEHAVIOUR : RELEASE

An important quality in a best friend is their manners. It's hard to be friends with someone who always pushes past you through doors, barges you out of the way to get to their dinner or snatches treats from your hand without being offered. Train your new friend to be the politest puppy in town with this etiquette lesson.

The release command can be used to:

- Get your puppy to wait at the other side of a door until you want them to come through.

- Get your puppy to wait patiently for their food until you tell them they can eat it.

- Get your puppy to stay in their crate when you open the door until you would like them to come out, instead of barging their way through.

1. Sit on the floor with your puppy and a few treats in your hand.

2. With your palm facing upward, show your puppy the treats.

3. If your puppy tries to take the treats, close your hand quickly so that they can't get them.

4. When your puppy has settled, show them the treat again with your palm facing upward. Close your hand if your puppy tries to take the treats again. You want your puppy to see the treats and not try to take them.

5. When you show your puppy the treat and they do not try to take it, use a release command and give your puppy the treat. My release command is, "OK!"

Ashleigh's Tip

Don't use your clicker for this skill because you want your puppy to listen to your release command and not the click.

Fine-tune

Once you have taught your puppy their release command like this, you can start adding it into different scenarios. A nice easy next step would be with their dinner.

1. Put your puppy's bowl down in front of them.

2. If your puppy rushes to get their dinner, take the bowl away quickly.

3. When your puppy waits calmly and does not rush to their bowl, use the release command to let them know they can have their dinner.

BASIC BEHAVIOUR : RECALL

Best friends are always there when you need them. Work on this with your puppy to make sure they come when you call.

Ashleigh's Tip

If this is a new skill for your puppy, begin your practice in your home where your puppy is comfortable and where there will be fewer things to distract them.

YOU WILL NEED:

- Treats
- Toys

1. Practise when your puppy is out of their crate and following you about your home. As soon as your puppy is distracted by something, run away.

2. Get your puppy's attention by making a fun sound. My go-to sound is rolling or clicking my tongue.

3. When your puppy comes to you, reward them with a treat or by playing with them with their favourite toy.

4. Once your puppy understands the recall noise in the house, head outside into your garden or an outside space they are familiar with. This will be more difficult as there will be more distractions.

Hide and seek

If your puppy starts to become distracted and stops paying attention to your recall noise, play hide and seek. I play hide and seek with my puppies a lot because it builds up their desire to want to come and find me. Try not to make it too hard for them. If you see them starting to look for you, give them a clue with your recall noise. Once they find you, give them lots of praise and play together.

Ashleigh's Tip

Switch between different rewards for your puppy to find out which is their favourite. Is it treats, toys or even an empty plastic bottle to play with? Whatever it is, use it! So, either play tuggy with them, or give them lots of treats while telling them they have done a good job. With my dogs, I usually switch between toys and treats as I want them to value them equally. This is so when I'm teaching either agility or trick training, I can use both rewards. Not all dogs will want to work for both, and that's OK! Every dog is different!

BASIC BEHAVIOUR: LEAD WALKING

Taking your puppy for a walk is great exercise for both of you and can be really good fun. Puppies love being out and are excited to explore the environment, but this doesn't mean they get to pull you everywhere they want to go. That's no fun for either of you. Follow these simple steps to make sure you and your best friend walk side by side.

Ashleigh's Tip

When I first get a puppy, I like to use a collar to teach them to not pull, but then I like to move on to using a small harness. This takes any pressure off their neck and is much more comfortable for them.

1. Take your puppy out for a walk on their lead.

2. If your puppy starts pulling on their lead, stop moving completely.

3. Wait for your puppy to stop pulling and come back to you.

4. Reward your dog with a treat or a loving stroke. Resume walking.

STICK WITH IT! This is a behaviour a lot of puppies and owners struggle with. With a lot of time and consistency, you can make sure you and your best friend are always in step.

5. Stop moving every time your dog starts to pull and reward them when they return to you. This teaches your dog that pulling and straining on their lead equals stopping, and that walking by your side with a loose lead means they can carry on moving.

Ashleigh's Tip

I don't always give my dogs treats for this as some dogs may learn that if they pull and then come back to you they will get a tasty treat, and pull more often.

BASIC BEHAVIOUR: EYE CONTACT

When you and your puppy have eye contact, it means you have your puppy's full attention and that they aren't distracted by anything that might be going on around you. Follow these steps to make sure you and your best friend always see eye to eye.

1. Sit in front of your puppy with a treat in each of your hands.

2. Hold your hands either side of your face. Your puppy will naturally look to each of your hands.

3. Wait until your puppy looks away from your hands and looks at your face. Try to remember which of your hands your puppy last looked at.

4. If your puppy last looked at your right hand, reward your puppy from your left hand and vice versa. This is so your dog doesn't anticipate their reward as it does not come from the hand they last looked at.

5. As your puppy starts offering the behaviour more quickly, hold off on giving them their reward to have longer eye contact.

Fine-tune

Once your puppy has mastered this behaviour at home where there aren't too many distractions, try it in other environments. With any behaviour there is no point trying to practise where there are lots of distractions when your puppy isn't sure what you are asking of them. If your puppy doesn't know what you want from them, they will not offer you the behaviour and therefore not get a reward. With no reward and lots of distractions, they may get bored and give up.

LEARNING TO GET ALONG

Once your puppy has practised their basic behaviours, you can move on to boundary games. To become best friends, you and puppy need to understand what to expect from one another. Dog training is all about setting boundaries and being consistent with how you teach them.

A puppy's cute and cuddly antics can be fun to begin with, but that can change quickly when they get a bit bigger and start to think they know best. You and your puppy will get along much better if you establish firm boundaries early on so that your puppy understands what is fun and what is off limits.

BOUNDARY GAME: CRATE FUN

Crate games teach your dog that their crate is a happy and safe place to be. It teaches your dog that even though there may be lots of exciting things happening around them, they have to stay in their crate until you tell them to leave. Crate training also helps to activate your dog's natural instinct to find a quiet and comfortable area when their environment gets too much for them.

1. Lead your puppy to their crate. Throw a puppy dog treat into the puppy crate. If your puppy follows the treat into the crate, press your clicker and throw in another treat as a reward. When your puppy comes out of the crate, repeat until you are sure your puppy has got the hang of it.

2. Lead your puppy to their crate. Hold off on throwing the first treat and wait to see if your puppy offers the behaviour to walk into the crate by themselves, if they do, click and reward. Repeat until you think your puppy has got the hang of it.

3. Lead your puppy to their crate. Use a command to instruct your puppy to go into its crate. Something simple and clear such as, "In your bed," is ideal. To help your puppy know what you expect, point to their crate when you say, "In your bed". If they go into their crate, click and reward. Repeat until you think your puppy has got the hang of it.

4. The last step is to start leaving your puppy in their crate. Still throw their treat into the crate when they walk in and start slowly building up the distance and time between going back and rewarding them. If possible, when you go back to them, reward them by throwing the treat into their crate without opening the door. This way your puppy is getting their reward but they won't be able to leave through the door or run past you by accident.

BOUNDARY GAME: SOFA SO GOOD

This fun game teaches your puppy that they can only go up on to your sofa when you say they can. This is important because if you don't teach them this straight away, your puppy will think they can go on the sofa whenever they choose. This becomes hard work when you have friends over who don't like dogs!

IMPORTANT: Wait until your puppy is at least six months old. It is not safe for very young puppies to jump up on to the sofa as they may hurt themselves.

YOU WILL NEED:

- Sofa
- Clicker
- Treats

1. Call your puppy to the sofa. Use a short, clear command such as "Up!" and pat or point at the sofa. If your puppy hops up on to the sofa, click the clicker and give them a treat.

2. To get your puppy off the sofa, use a command such as "Off!" and point to the ground. If your puppy hops off the sofa and puts all four feet on the ground, click the clicker and give them a treat.

3. Repeat regularly until you are sure your puppy has the hang of it.

The "Off" command can be used for other situations too, such as when a puppy jumps up on someone or puts their front paws up on the kitchen counter. Once they have left their position and all four paws are on the ground, click and reward.

Ashleigh's Tip

Mix up your rewards. Rather than give a treat every time, try offering a toy and verbal rewards such as "Good!" or "Well done!" This will stop your puppy always assuming they get treated for every little thing they do.

Section 5:

TRICKIER TRAINING

Now that your puppy understands basic behaviours and how to play boundary games, and you know all about how to care for your puppy, it is time to move on to some trickier training.

Just like people, dogs are more likely to learn if they are having fun. It's like reading a boring book: you end up reading the same page over and over again but find you keep switching off and nothing goes in. But when that same information is presented in a fun way, by a teacher you like or on a television show, all of the information sticks in your mind and you can't wait to learn more. And just like people, all dogs are individuals. The sign of a good dog trainer is adapting to the dog you have in front of you, as not all dogs are going to fit one training method or technique.

EASY TRICKS

I love trick training with my dogs, as it helps them and me to understand their bodies better by seeing how they move and what their strengths and weaknesses are. While these tricks may seem simple, they are very important. Easy tricks are stepping stones to more complicated skills. A spin in front of you on the ground can progress into your dog spinning on an object like a box.

Trick training is a great way to:

- Strengthen the bond with your dog.

- Stimulate your dog mentally, and tire them out more than a walk.

- Impress your friends and family!

Sully likes to do everything at a million miles per hour, so I need to be as calm as possible when teaching him something new. However, as well as wanting to do everything quickly, his confidence can drop just as fast, so alongside being calm, I also need to give him lots of encouragement. This will include me quietly telling him he's good, or using the command word of "Yes!" To Sully, "Yes!" means that what he is doing is correct but that he hasn't quite completed it to a standard that warrants a treat reward.

Vi, on the other hand, likes to think about things. He is a perfectionist and always wants to get things right for me. You can really see him using his brain. This means that when he is learning something new, he is slightly slower. Vi has taught me to be more patient as a trainer. I have to adapt my training to him. It doesn't mean that Vi isn't as smart as Sully, or isn't enjoying it as much, it's just how he learns. Vi's way of learning actually makes him less likely to pick up bad habits and even learn things quicker. Once Vi is confident with a trick or behaviour, he then puts more speed and enthusiasm into it.

EASY TRICK : IN A SPIN

This is a really fun trick — here's how you can teach your dog to spin clockwise and anti-clockwise in front of you.

68

Ashleigh's Tip

Make sure you work one direction a few times before you move onto the other direction. I find if people go from one way straight into the other way, their dog starts to expect this pattern instead of waiting for you to tell them what to do.

1. Stand with your dog in front of you.

2. Decide which direction you would like your puppy to spin. If you are sending your dog round clockwise, put a treat in your left hand.

IF YOUR DOG IS STANDING:

 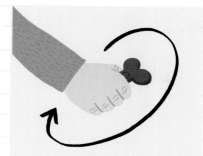

3. Hold the hand with the treat on your puppy's nose so that they can smell it.

4. Move your arm in a tight circle and wait for your puppy to follow your hand.

IF YOUR DOG IS SITTING:

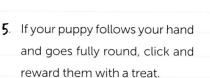

5. If your puppy follows your hand and goes fully round, click and reward them with a treat.

3. Take a step back and call your puppy to you. As soon as your puppy comes towards you, put your hand close to their nose so they can smell the treat.

4. Move your arm in a tight circle and wait for your puppy to follow your hand.

5. If your puppy follows your hand and goes fully round, click and reward them with a treat.

6. When sending your dog anti-clockwise, put your puppy's treat in your right hand and practise exactly what you did before but going in the opposite direction.

Fine-tune

Once your dog is moving round in those circles smoothly, you can start to take your hands away a little more.

Repeat the steps above, but keep your hand above your puppy's head and make the movement much smaller. You may find your puppy starts to spin tighter and quicker – this is exactly what we want. This is also the point where you can add in commands. Decide which direction you want your puppy to spin and choose a command for that direction. I use spin for clockwise and twist for anti-clockwise. Keeping your commands separate now, will help prevent any confusion later.

Ashleigh's Tip

If your puppy is finishing with their bottom facing to the side, they haven't completed a full spin. To help them complete their spin and finish straighter, I send them around for their spin and take a small step back as they come around so they step forward towards me. Hold off on that reward until they are nice and straight.

EASY TRICK : NOSE -HAND TOUCH

Dogs love to explore the world with their noses! I really like this trick because it is also another way that I recall my dogs without saying their names. It turns into another game of "How quickly can I get back and nose touch to get my reward?"

1. With multiple treats in one hand, hold your other hand five centimetres away from your puppy's nose with your palm facing it.

2. Wait until your puppy sniffs your palm or moves their head towards your palm. As soon as they do, click and reward by placing a treat from the other hand into the hand you wanted them to touch with their nose. This reinforces the behaviour that you want.

Ashleigh's Tip

Multiple treats are best so you don't have to stop to get more every time you reward. This means there is less of a chance for your puppy to get bored.

3. As your puppy gets better at this skill, start adding a command and extend the amount of time your puppy touches your palm with their nose for. Build up the amount of time slowly by holding off the reward when they nose touch the first time, and only rewarding when they offer the nose touch for the second time. Your puppy may even get a little frustrated and start adding more pressure to their nose touches to make sure they get their reward.

4. When your puppy gets the hang of touching their nose to your palm twice, the gap between the nose touches should become shorter. Work on perfecting your rewarding so that when your puppy offers you a longer nose touch than normal, you can quickly bonus reward that behaviour.

Ashleigh's Tip

Practise changing the hand your puppy's nose touches, so they don't get used to you always using the same hand. Make sure when your puppy is nose touching, you're keeping a nice solid hand for them.

EASY TRICK : LEG WEAVE

Perfecting this skill may take as much practice from you as it does for your puppy.

This trick gets your puppy bending their body, which is great if you're thinking about doing agility when they're older!

1. With a few treats in each hand, stand with your legs shoulder width apart and your dog sitting or standing in front of you. Having a few treats in each hand means you won't distract your puppy by switching the treats from one hand to the other.

2. Wrap one of your hands around the back of your leg, so that your hand is positioned between your legs and in front of your puppy. Call your puppy through your legs and around the back of your legs until they are standing beside you. Click and reward your puppy with a treat.

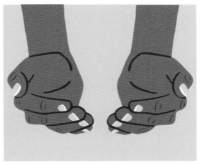

3. Once your puppy has completed their first weave, wrap your other hand around the back of your other leg and call your puppy through again, rewarding once they have gone through your legs, around the back and then reached the side of your opposite leg.

4. Repeat this until you run out of treats in each hand.

Fine-tune

When you've worked on this for a while and you think your puppy is starting to understand, start asking for more leg weaves for less reward.

To do this, do not reward your puppy after completing the first leg weave. Instead, put your arm behind your other leg to command your puppy into the second leg weave. Reward your puppy once this leg weave is complete.

Continue to practise, rewarding every second leg weave. This is a good time to start using a command.

As your puppy begins to master this skill, reward less often and expect your puppy to rely more on your command than the position of your arms. Instead of wrapping your arm around the back of your leg, keep your arm by your side to show your puppy which leg you want them to weave around. Try doing three or four leg weaves before you offer a reward.

Make sure you offer your puppy lots of encouragement to make sure they know they are doing a good job.

EASY TRICK : ON THE BOX

The aim of this trick is to get your puppy to place their two front paws up on to a box. Make sure that the object you are using is sturdy enough to take the weight of your puppy, as we don't want it to topple over or collapse and scare them. For smaller puppies, I'd recommend an old sweet tin (this might need something inside to weigh it down so that it won't slide when your puppy puts their paws on to it!). For larger dogs, I'd recommend a stool or a large box.

1. Put the object or box you want your puppy to put their paws on, on to the floor. Put some treats on top of the box. Your puppy will have to approach the box and touch it to receive their reward. This introduces your puppy to the object and shows them it is something fun and not scary.

2. When your puppy is completely happy with going near the box, try and get them to place their paws on to it. Hold a treat in your hand just above the box, high enough so that your puppy has to step their front paws on to the box in order to reach it.

Ashleigh's Tip

Some puppies might find this a little scary, so try to be very calm and not make sudden movements when they are near the box.

3. When your puppy steps on to the box, even if it just with one paw, reward them and give them lots of praise.

4. Once your puppy has mastered putting one paw up on to the box, repeat the practice, but hold off giving your puppy a reward until you see both paws up on the box.

5. When your puppy is happy to put both paws up on the box every time, introduce a command. I use "Box!"

Fine-tune

If your puppy seems happy with their front paws up on the box, see if you can get them to stay there for a few seconds before you offer them a reward. This will take a bit of practice and require your puppy to learn a bit of patience.

Ashleigh's Tip

You might need to be patient, too. Some puppies absolutely love this trick and try to jump all over the box, whereas some other puppies are more timid, and may find it a little scary.

EASY TRICK : BETWEEN POSITION

This skill requires your dog to stand between your legs. I love this trick and find I use it a lot in everyday life with my dogs. I use it with them for agility and start line waits, and I use it out on walks if I want them to come into a solid position and just wait there. It's simple and very useful.

1. Stand with your feet shoulder-width apart with your dog sitting or standing in front of you. With a treat in each of your hands, use one hand to guide your puppy around the back of your leg.

2. Once your puppy is behind you, reach between your legs from the front with your other hand. Guide your dog through your legs until they are positioned between them. Reward this position with a treat from both hands.

3. Once you've rewarded your puppy throw a treat forward to bring your dog out of their position from between your legs.

4. As your puppy becomes more confident practising this skill with you using two hands to guide them, try it using one hand. Use one hand to send your puppy around the back of your legs and reward them from the front once they are between them.

5. When your puppy is comfortable performing this skill with you using one hand, start using a command. I use, "Between!" Also start holding off when you treat them to see if they will stay in that position – to begin with just for a few seconds and then start building it up.

Fine-tune

If your dog follows your command and stands between your legs, try asking them to sit. This will be a nice solid position for puppy, and will make them less likely to leave before you release.

Ashleigh's Tip

When throwing the treat forward to release your dog, make sure you use their clear release command as well. Try to just teach your puppy to go around the same leg each time for this trick. This will make it easier and more consistent for the dogs. I always send my dogs around my right leg.

TRICKS, TRICKS AND MORE TRICKS!

Being a good dog trainer also involves being creative and thinking outside of the box. As you learn more about your dog's strengths, you will be able to use them to your advantage. Once your puppy knows their basic behaviours and tricks, why not start thinking about other tricks you could teach them. These could either be really easy things like giving a paw, or taking a trick they already know like spins and making it more advanced, such as asking for multiple spins or getting them to spin on a box.

TRICK-TRAINING MUSTS

While all puppies are different kinds of learners, there are some things I always try to keep the same when teaching my dogs new things.

Time

Keep your training sessions short and sweet. I can achieve more in a short ten-minute training session with my dogs than I can in an hour session. This is because for those ten minutes I have my dog's full attention, which keeps them fresh and wanting to learn. To keep the session to ten minutes, I set a timer on my phone. When the timer goes off, I finish the trick I am working on and end the session. And if you're going to do two training sessions in one day, make sure you leave a good few hours in between each one.

Plan

Plan your training sessions before you start. I try to plan before each training session so I'm not stopping and starting with my puppy. The more I stop, the more likely they will get bored and distracted. I begin with an easy behaviour to engage their brain, such as a sit, or an eye contact game. Then, I will work on a slightly harder trick, something that they are yet to master or something that is brand new to them. To finish, I like to do something fun like a game of hide and seek or recall game. When you play games like these, you are still training your puppy, but they are having so much fun they don't realize they are learning.

Change it Up

Make each training session slightly different. I try to vary the behaviours I work on with my dogs, as I don't want the sessions to become repetitive, but I try not to make them so different that each session becomes information overload. As well as teaching new behaviours, I often revise tricks that my puppy knows and understands. This builds the puppy's confidence and makes sure they don't forget old tricks.

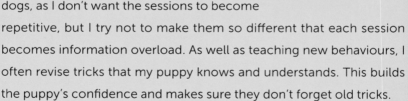

ASHLEIGH'S SCHEDULE:
Eliza

Monday . . . . TWO TEN-MINUTE SESSIONS (AM AND PM)

SESSION 1

- Sit
- Nose touch
- Recalls

SESSION 2

- Recalls
- Spins
- Nose touch

Tuesday . . . . TWO TEN-MINUTE SESSIONS (AM AND PM)

SESSION 1

- Down
- On the box
- Crate games

SESSION 2

- Repeat session 1 from yesterday!

Have Fun!

NOTE:
DON'T FORGET TO SET THE TIMER!

Make sure you enjoy your sessions with your puppy. If you're not having fun, then your puppy won't be having fun! Your best friend knows when you are faking your emotions and you can't pretend with them.

If I'm having a bad day or I don't feel well, I don't train my dogs. It would be pointless as I wouldn't be in the right frame of mind. When I don't feel good, I may not have the patience that I would normally have. Instead, I might just spend some quality time with them, whether that's just sitting having a cuddle or going out for a walk together. The special bond I have with my dogs is not just the result of training, it's also made by enjoying each other's company and spending precious time together.

Learning FUN-damentals

Have you ever been in a class with a really boring teacher, who drones on so much that you don't take anything in? Well, our puppies can see us like that if we aren't fun and engaging. The world is a new and exciting place to your puppy, and there are a lot of distractions out there. It's your job to be more interesting and exciting than every single one of them. This might include you running around like a crazy person or being loud and noisy, but it will keep your puppy engaged. It all comes back to that special word: fun!

YOUR PUPPY'S PROGRESS

When you first bring your puppy home, they may seem to struggle with even their basic behaviours, but with a few short training sessions, you will soon see how quickly they learn and how happy they are to play these games with you.

As you and your puppy get to know one another better, you can start to decide what you want from your friendship. Do you want a playmate who is fun and excited when you want to play, and knows a few tricks but knows how to calm down when you need them to? Or, do you want a competition-ready agility champion who is able to follow even the most difficult commands?

To achieve either of these perfect puppy outcomes, it helps to set a few goals.

FRIENDSHIP GOALS

I set goals for all of my dogs and track their progress on their very own progress charts. As I have said before, all puppies and dogs are different. Your friend's dog may be really good at a sit, whereas yours stares at you blankly when you give that command. Your dog might be great at recall, whereas their dog never comes back to them. This is why it is important to set goals that are unique to you and your dog and what you want from your relationship.

I break my goals up into two categories: long-term goals and short-term goals.

LONG-TERM GOALS

To make a long-term goal for you and your puppy, think about where you see your puppy in a year's time. Do you see yourself being able to go to a park, let your dog off of the lead and know they will come back as soon as you call them? Or are your dreams a little bigger, such as competing in trick training or agility with them? It doesn't matter about the goal itself: what matters is the time, effort and planning you put into achieving it.

Vi's long-term goals

My long-term goal for Vi is for him to be a Crufts Champion and for him to be happy to compete in all of the big competitions, but at only one-and-a-half years old, that is a little way off.

ONE YEAR FROM NOW:

☐ **To be able to compete in agility competitions.**

☐ **To be confident and happy running with me and having fun.**

Hopefully, when Vi has completed this long-term goal, then I can start thinking about his next long-term goal of qualifying for big events.

TWO YEARS FROM NOW:

In agility we have a grading system, a little like you have at school. We have grades one to seven in the UK, one being the lowest and seven being the championship level. Our two-year goal will be to work our way through these grades. Along the way we will have courses or training sequences that will highlight our weaknesses and strengths. This is good because it will show me what we will need to work on going forward.

THREE YEARS FROM NOW:

I would like our three-year long-term goal to be running in our first big final. We have a few big finals in this country like Crufts, Olympia and Championships Final. I think this will be a realistic

goal for him; it's a tough goal to meet, but I'm not just aiming for one particular event so there's slightly less pressure.

For all of Vi's goals, whether long- or short-term, my biggest goals are to have fun together, make sure Vi is always happy and that we keep up all of the training we have done throughout his life. Whether that's basic behaviours, or trickier ones.

Sully's long-term goals

Sully is eight years old and has smashed a lot of the long-term goals I set for him! However, I would say that Sully's long-term goals are to keep up with all of the tricks and training that he already knows. As dogs get older, sometimes we let things slip a little, which could lead to our dog forgetting basic manners or tricks. I also want to keep teaching him new tricks that he's never learned before. This takes some thinking outside of the box for me as he knows a LOT of tricks! Also, brushing up on tricks that he's always struggled with, like walking on his back legs where he wants to do it so fast but he loses control!

GET YOUR OWN GOALS

Think about what long-term goals you would like to set for you and your puppy. You can keep a record of them here!

NAME: . . . . 'S LONG-TERM GOALS

ONE-YEAR GOAL: . . . .

TWO-YEAR GOAL: . . . .

THREE-YEAR GOAL: . . . .

Long-term goals may take a bit of thought. They aren't goals that you can just think of and then go and do. Long-term goals need a plan for how you will achieve them.

SHORT-TERM GOALS

Once you have decided your long-term goals for your puppy, now you can think about how you can use your short-term goals to make your dreams for your puppy a reality. Short-term goals are behaviours and tasks that you want them to complete on a day-to-day, week-in week-out basis. Perfect short-term goals include perfecting tricks that are still a bit messy, and not letting basic manners and behaviours slide.

Sully's short-term goals

☐ Keep training tricks he already knows to keep them fresh in his mind.

☐ Keep fit, so that he is ready for competition. This includes agility training and trick training every other day.

☐ Introduce new tricks he has not done before to keep training exciting.

Vi's short-term goals

Vi's goals are different to Sully's because Vi is younger and isn't as experienced as Sully.

☐ Keep training basic behaviours, such as release command when it comes to food or walking through doors.

☐ Work on basic tricks until he knows them 100%.

☐ Work on recall, especially when he is around exciting dogs and he wants to run with them!

With a new puppy, my short-term goals include:

☐ Encouraging them to engage with me.

☐ Introducing the clicker.

☐ Practising basic behaviours such as sit, crate games and eye contact.

☐ Establishing that I am their best friend and the most fun person to be around!

SKILLS CHART

Something that I find really helps me to keep on track is keeping a record of my puppy's progress. Then I can see at a glance what my puppy can do and what they might be struggling with.

Use the chart below to jot down when you introduce behaviours and tricks and how your puppy is progressing. This can help when training isn't quite going to plan, as you will be able to see just how far you and your puppy have come!

Skill/Behaviour/Trick	DATE		
	Started	Halfway there	Completed it

BASIC BEHAVIOURS

Sit			
Release			
Recall			
Lead Walking			
Eye Contact			

BOUNDARY GAMES

Crate Fun			
Sofa So Good			

EASY TRICKS

In a Spin			
Leg Weave			
Nose-Hand touch			
On the Box			
Between Position			

STAY FLEXIBLE

Setting goals is great because it means you have a clear image in your mind on where you want to be with your puppy and what you want to be able to do together, but you need to stay flexible, too. Training doesn't always work out the way you want, or expect it to. This is why you need to be patient. Puppies have personalities just like people. They can be anxious or bold, busy or lazy, and like people they all learn at different speeds.

When a training session isn't going how you want it to, it can seem like your puppy is purposely trying to make you angry or sad, but they aren't. All puppies want to do is please you. Your puppy might just need more time. This is when you need to remember the positive things you and your puppy have achieved.

While you might not always reach your goals when you hoped to, sometimes you may reach different goals and learn skills you thought would have been a lot more difficult. Just remember, you are having great fun with your puppy and you're learning so many new things together, and that is the main thing.

Be a show-off!

Make sure you show off your puppy's new learned behaviours to your friends and family to help you keep motivated. You may think that your puppy isn't learning as quickly as you would like them to, or that the skills and behaviours you are working on aren't very impressive, but other people will love them!

A Final Note from Ashleigh!

I have been training dogs for a very long time, and trust me, I'm not perfect at training and none of my dogs are perfectly trained.

When you see me performing or competing with Sully, Eliza or Vi, you might think it looks easy, but it is not. If training dogs was easy, everyone would be able to do it, and all dogs would be able to walk on their back legs and be perfectly behaved. Some people may be more natural at training dogs than others. But even natural or experienced dog trainers still have to learn how to work with each individual dog and how to best teach them new skills. Good trainers have to adapt their training to dogs that may be struggling with a particular behaviour and practise behaviours they have already taught to keep them fresh. This, on top of being consistent with everything you do and being a fun companion to your dog, can make it sound very difficult. But it is worth it. I've become the trainer I am today with a lot of time, effort, dedication, a few tears, but also a lot of fun.

A dog will love you unconditionally and they will greet you at the door excitedly even if you just popped out for five minutes. They're a constant companion that will be there for you at your highest and lowest times. They will make you laugh with their quirky unique ways, and they will get you out and about meeting new people that love dogs just as much as you do. They will teach you things that you never even knew you needed to learn.

A dog can be your best friend, and if you give them the time and attention they deserve, they will give you their whole lives.

INDEX